You're supposed to lead, CHARLIE BROWN

by Charles M. Schulz

Selected cartoons from
DOGS DON'T EAT DESSERT

FAWCETT CREST • NEW YORK

A Fawcett Crest Book
Published by Ballantine Books
Contents of Book: PEANUTS® Comic Strips by Charles M. Schulz
                    Copyright © 1985, 1987 by United Feature Syndicate, Inc.

Library of Congress Catalog Card Number: 86-63046

ISBN 0-449-21488-5

This book comprises a portion of DOGS DON'T EAT DESSERT and is
reprinted by arrangement with Pharos Books.

Manufactured in the United States of America

First Ballantine Books Edition: July 1988

You're supposed to lead, CHARLIE BROWN

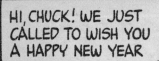

HI, CHUCK! WE JUST CALLED TO WISH YOU A HAPPY NEW YEAR

DO YOU STILL LOVE ME, CHUCK?

1-85

MARCIE WANTS TO KNOW IF YOU STILL LOVE HER, TOO, CHUCK...

I'M SORRY...I'M NOT HERE ANY MORE...I'VE SUDDENLY BECOME A RECORDING!

PEANUTS.

featuring

"Good ol' Charlie Brown"

by SCHULZ

YOU WON, SIR!

WON WHAT?

I JUST HEARD THAT YOUR ESSAY ON WHAT YOU DID DURING CHRISTMAS VACATION WON THE "ALL-CITY SCHOOL ESSAY CONTEST"

1-7-85

YOU WROTE ABOUT LOOKING AT THE CLOUDS, REMEMBER? ANYWAY, YOU WON..CONGRATULATIONS!

DON'T WIPE YOUR TEARS AWAY WITH YOUR FRENCH FRIES, SIR

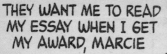
THEY WANT ME TO READ MY ESSAY WHEN I GET MY AWARD, MARCIE

I'LL PROBABLY HAVE TO DRESS UP, AND MAYBE EVEN CHANGE MY HAIR STYLE...

1-10-85

SEE IF YOU LIKE IT THIS WAY, SIR..

ONLY IF I WANT TO GO DISGUISED AS A DANDELION

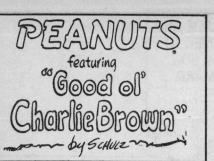

PEANUTS
featuring
"Good ol' Charlie Brown"
— by SCHULZ —

GO AHEAD.. THROW IT!

THERE'S TWO OF US AND ONLY ONE OF YOU...

I HAVE BEEN ASKED TO READ THE ESSAY THAT I WROTE ABOUT MY CHRISTMAS VACATION..

PERHAPS, HOWEVER, A FEW WORDS MIGHT BE IN ORDER HERE TO TELL...

HURRY UP, AND READ IT!!

MARCIE!

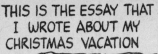

➤

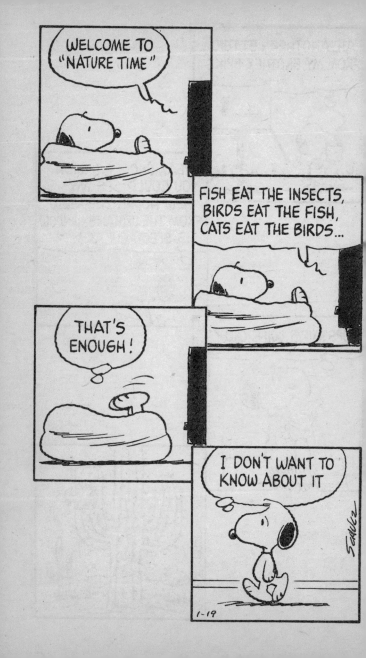

HIPPITY-
HOP

BUNNIES HIPPITY-HOP...
DOGS DON'T HIPPITY-HOP..

1-21

1-23

HOW CAN YOU TELL WHICH BOOT GOES ON WHICH FOOT?

I HATE ZIPPERS! OH, HOW I HATE ZIPPERS!

2-2

AND MITTENS! HOW CAN YOU TELL WHERE THE THUMBS GO?!

I WASN'T MADE FOR WINTER!

HERE'S THE WORLD FAMOUS SURGEON OUT FOR HIS MORNING JOG...

2-7

IT'S RAINING AND THE WIND IS BLOWING..

WHAT AM I DOING OUT HERE?

I COULD BE IN A NICE WARM OPERATING ROOM!

PEANUTS

featuring "Good ol' Charlie Brown"

by Schulz

THIS IS A VALENTINE I BOUGHT FOR THAT LITTLE RED-HAIRED GIRL...

I WANT TO GO OVER TO HER HOUSE, AND GIVE IT TO HER, BUT I THINK I'D BE TOO NERVOUS TO DO IT WITHOUT PRACTICE...

IT'S ALL VERY STRANGE..

YOU CAN BE WALKING ALONG NOT THINKING OF ANYTHING IN PARTICULAR

2-11

SUDDENLY, YOU'RE REMINDED OF A LOST LOVE...

SCHULZ

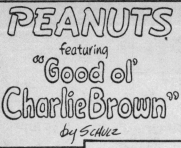

Dear Sweetheart,

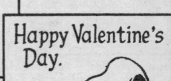

Happy Valentine's Day.

Do you still love me?

2-14

Good.

WHAT DID YOU PUT DOWN FOR NUMBER THREE, MARCIE, TRUE OR FALSE?

TRUE, SIR! TRUE BLUE! AS TRUE AS I LIVE! TRUE AS STARS ABOVE!

MORE TRUE THAN LOVE TO ME! OH, 'TIS TRUE, 'TIS TRUE! TENDER AND TRUE!

I THINK I'LL SKIP THAT ONE

2-15

WHY, MAY I ASK, ARE YOU BUILDING A USELESS ROCK WALL?

I DISCOVERED THAT I HAVE THE ABILITY TO PICK UP A ROCK, AND TO CARRY IT FROM ONE PLACE TO ANOTHER

2-21

THEN, I DISCOVERED THAT I COULD PILE THEM UP, AND MAKE A ROCK WALL.. IT'S UGLY AND USELESS, BUT WHO CARES?

WHEN YOU'RE DONE, YOU CAN MAKE A SECOND WALL WITH THE ROCKS IN YOUR HEAD!

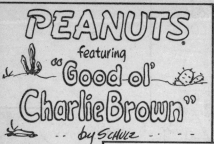

⟶

WHAT'S THIS?

A BAG OF READY-MIX MORTAR

YOU SHOULD CEMENT THESE ROCKS TOGETHER.. IT'LL MAKE A BETTER WALL..ALL WE HAVE TO DO IS ADD WATER...

OKAY, TURN ON THE WATER! BRING THAT HOSE OVER HERE!

2-23

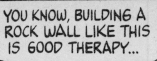

YOU KNOW, BUILDING A ROCK WALL LIKE THIS IS GOOD THERAPY...

EVEN IF IT'S A USELESS WALL, IT HELPS JUST TO BE DOING SOMETHING

I HAVE A FEELING THAT WORKING ON THIS ROCK WALL MAY EVEN HELP ME TO GIVE UP MY BLANKET...

I'M GLAD TO HEAR YOU SAY THAT BECAUSE I CEMENTED YOUR BLANKET INTO THE WALL!

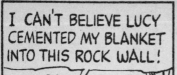

I CAN'T BELIEVE LUCY CEMENTED MY BLANKET INTO THIS ROCK WALL!

YOU DON'T NEED YOUR BLANKET ANY MORE..YOU SAID SO YOURSELF...THIS ROCK WALL IS YOUR THERAPY..

2-26

EVERY TIME YOU HAVE A LITTLE STRESS IN YOUR LIFE, YOU CAN COME OUT HERE AND ADD A FEW ROCKS TO YOUR WALL...

THERE AREN'T THAT MANY ROCKS IN THE WORLD!!

SCHULZ

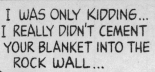

I WAS ONLY KIDDING... I REALLY DIDN'T CEMENT YOUR BLANKET INTO THE ROCK WALL...

I DID GIVE HALF OF IT TO THE KID NEXT DOOR, HOWEVER... HE NEEDED IT..

YOU GAVE HALF OF MY BLANKET TO THE KID NEXT DOOR?!!

ONLY THE MIDDLE HALF!

2/27

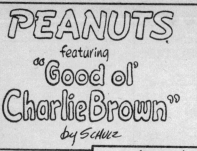

3-3

HE SAID ALL THE ENLISTED MEN WERE ISSUED TWO PAIRS OF SHOES, BUT A LOT OF THE MEN WORE ONLY ONE PAIR SO THEY COULD KEEP THE OTHER PAIR SHINED AND LOOKING NICE UNDER THEIR BUNKS...

BATTALION HEADQUARTERS DECIDED THAT THE MEN SHOULD ALTERNATE SHOES EACH DAY, AND TO MAKE SURE THEY DID, THE MEN HAD TO LACE THEIR SHOES IN A CERTAIN WAY...

ONE DAY THEY HAD TO WEAR THE SHOES WHICH HAD THE LACES CROSSED, AND THE NEXT DAY THEY HAD TO WEAR THE SHOES WHICH HAD THE LACES GOING STRAIGHT ACROSS...

HOW DID THEY EVER WIN THE WAR?

IN A GOOD CONVERSATION, ONE PERSON TALKS WHILE THE OTHER LISTENS

THEN THAT PERSON TALKS WHILE THE FIRST PERSON LISTENS...

I LIKE TALKING.. I HATE LISTENING

I REALIZE THAT

3-2

WHAT ?

IT SAYS HERE THIS IS THE TENTH ANNUAL "TINY TOTS" CONCERT

YOU KNOW WHAT?

WHAT?

I HATE BEING CALLED A "TINY TOT"!

EVERY TIME WE COME TO ONE OF THESE CONCERTS, THEY PLAY "PETER AND THE WOLF"

THEY MUST THINK WE DON'T UNDERSTAND ANYTHING ELSE

DON'T YOU LIKE "PETER AND THE WOLF"?

I DON'T KNOW..I'VE NEVER UNDERSTOOD IT!

WHY DOES THE CONDUCTOR HAVE THAT STICK, MARCIE?

THAT'S A BATON, SIR... HE USES IT TO LEAD THE ORCHESTRA...

3-6

I DON'T THINK HE NEEDS IT...

THEY ALL SEEM PRETTY WELL-BEHAVED TO ME..

THEY TOOK OUR CLASS TO A "TINY TOTS" CONCERT TODAY..IT WAS IN A BIG AUDITORIUM DOWNTOWN

THE AUDITORIUM HAD LONG AISLES WITH A RED CARPET...

WHAT WAS YOUR FAVORITE PART OF THE CONCERT?

WALKING ON THE RED CARPET!

3-8

PEANUTS

featuring "Good ol' Charlie Brown"

by SCHULZ

IF I CATCH THIS BALL, WE'LL WIN OUR FIRST GAME OF THE SEASON..

A POP FLY!

I GOT IT! IT'S ALL MINE!

3-10

PLEASE LET ME CATCH IT! PLEASE LET ME BE THE HERO! PLEASE LET ME CATCH IT! PLEASE!

HERE'S A CUTE SWEATER, MARCIE..IT HAS LITTLE SHEEPS ALL OVER IT.... YOU SHOULD BUY IT...

I WONDER IF THEY'RE REALLY SHEEP...

MA'AM, HOW DO I KNOW THAT THESE AREN'T WOLVES IN SHEEP'S CLOTHING?

YOU'RE A SMART SHOPPER, MARCIE

Sale

AND I REMEMBER HOW GREEN IT USED TO BE IN THE SUMMER, AND THEN IN THE FALL IT CHANGED TO THE MOST BEAUTIFUL COLORS...

AND THERE WAS ONE PARTICULAR BRANCH..IT HAD A WONDERFUL CURVE TO IT, AND ALL THE BIRDS USED TO LOVE TO SIT ON IT, AND SING...

IT MAY BE GONE NOW, BUT AT LEAST YOU HAVE THOSE MEMORIES..YOU KNOW THAT YOU WERE BORN AND RAISED IN A VERY SPECIAL TREE...

ACTUALLY, I DON'T REMEMBER IT AT ALL.. I CAN'T TELL ONE TREE FROM ANOTHER!

SCHULZ

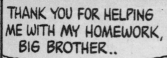

A History of
the World.

3-15

Volcanoes erupted.
Oceans boiled.

The universe was in
a turmoil.

Then came the
dog.

DO YOU MIND IF I ASK YOU SOMETHING?

WHAT DO YOU REALLY THINK THE CHANCES ARE THAT YOU AND I WILL GET MARRIED SOMEDAY?

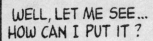

WELL, LET ME SEE... HOW CAN I PUT IT?

3-18

WHEN SOMEONE DOESN'T KNOW HOW TO PUT IT, YOU KNOW YOU'VE BEEN PUT!

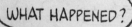

IT'S A MEDICAL FACT THAT BREATHING THROUGH YOUR MOUTH CAN CHANGE YOUR FACE...

3-21

ALLOWING FORTY RUNS IN THE FIRST INNING CAN CHANGE YOUR WHOLE BODY!

PEANUTS

featuring "Good ol' Charlie Brown"

by SCHULZ

NO, MA'AM

I'M SO ASHAMED OF MYSELF

3-24

I TOLD THE TEACHER I DIDN'T HAVE MY HOMEWORK DONE BECAUSE I WASN'T FEELING WELL LAST NIGHT..

ACTUALLY, I WAS WATCHING TV...NOW, I'LL BE PUNISHED WITH BAD LUCK... OR SOMEBODY IN OUR FAMILY WILL HAVE BAD LUCK...

YOU'RE JUST SUPERSTITIOUS

NO ONE COULD REALLY BELIEVE THAT SOMEBODY IN YOUR FAMILY WOULD HAVE BAD LUCK BECAUSE OF SOMETHING YOU DID...

BONK

HAS MY SISTER BEEN LYING AGAIN?!

SCHULZ

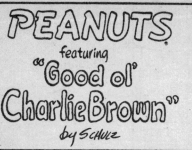

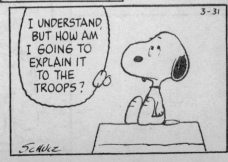

THE MEETING OF THE CACTUS CLUB WILL COME TO ORDER

FIRST WE'LL HAVE A REPORT FROM OUR ENTERTAINMENT COMMITTEE...

WHEE!

3-28

THANK YOU, ENTERTAINMENT COMMITTEE

4-2

ALL MY LIFE I WANTED TO BE AN ONLY CHILD... I HAD A GOOD THING GOING 'TIL YOU CAME..

LITTLE BROTHERS SPOIL EVERYTHING..LITTLE BROTHERS ARE A BOTHER AND A NUISANCE...

4-3

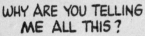

WHY ARE YOU TELLING ME ALL THIS?

THERE'S NOTHING GOOD ON TV!

SORRY I'M LATE, MA'AM

OUR DIGITAL CLOCK STOPPED...

4-5

YES, MA'AM, WE HAVE ANOTHER CLOCK..

I CAN'T READ IT, THOUGH..IT HAS HANDS

SCHULZ

I ALWAYS WEAR MY CAP TO BED ON THE NIGHT BEFORE A BIG GAME...

I GUESS IT'S JUST A SUPERSTITION

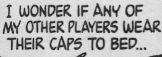

I WONDER IF ANY OF MY OTHER PLAYERS WEAR THEIR CAPS TO BED...

SCHULZ 4/10

PEANUTS

featuring
"Good ol' Charlie Brown"
by SCHULZ

WHAT DO YOU HAVE THERE?

LAUNDRY DETERGENT

→

I DECIDED I HAVE TO LEARN TO DO SOME THINGS FOR MYSELF...

IT'S RIDICULOUS FOR A MAN NOT TO KNOW HOW TO DO HIS OWN LAUNDRY!

I AGREE

RATS!

WHAT'S THE PROBLEM?

4-14

HOW DO I GET THE SHIRT INTO THE BOTTLE?

I'VE DECIDED TO BECOME BEGUILING

4-16

ON THE OTHER HAND..

IF I'M NOT BEGUILING BY THE TIME I'M TWELVE, FORGET IT!